Mah Jongg 2013

How To Play & Win

By Claire Fine

Copyright © 2013 Claire Fine
All rights reserved.

ISBN-13: 978-1-938886-78-2
ISBN-10: 193888678X

Table of Contents

Introduction..**1**

Who, What, Where, and When

What you Need to Play

How this book is Organized

> Part I *The Equipment*
> Part II *The Game*
> Part III *The Rules*
> Part IV *Setting up a Hand*
> Part V *The Charleston*
> Part VI *Strategy*
> Part VII *Points to Ponder*
> Part VIII *2013 Card Hands*
> Part IX *2013 Card Hand Switches*
> Part X *2013 Card Quizzes*

Part I *THE EQUIPMENT*..............................**5**

Chapter 1: The Mah Jongg Set.....................7

> Suits
> Dragons
> Winds
> Flowers
> Jokers

Chapter 2: The Mah Jongg Card.................11

    Know the Card
    Organization
    Hand Categories
    Exposed Hands
    Concealed Hands
    Colors
    Pungs, Kongs, Quints, and Sextets
    Dragons
    Use of Jokers
    Fine print
    Hand Values

Part II *THE GAME*..19

Chapter 3: Getting Started........................21

    Setting up the Walls
    Choosing East
    Throw of the Dice
    The Charleston
    First Round
    Second Round
    Stealing
    Courtesy

Chapter 4: Game Play................................25

    Order of Play
    Order of Walls
    Drawing the Tiles
    The Charleston
    Picking and Discarding

Calling Tiles:

> *For Exposure*
> *For Mah Jongg*

Joker Exchanges
Mah Jongg Declaration

Part III *THE RULES*...................................29

Chapter 5: Sequence of Play......................31

Chapter 6: Called Tiles............................33

When to Call
Order of play (after a call)

Chapter 7: Dead Hands...........................35

Declaring a Player dead
Declaring a Player dead in error
Exchanging Jokers from a dead hand's exposures
Mah Jongg declared in error

Chapter 8: Discard/Exposure Rules...........39

Naming a tile still in one's hand
Touching a future tile and calling simultaneously
Exposing tiles
Calling a misnamed tile for exposure
Calling a misnamed tile for Mah Jongg

Part IV *SETTING UP A HAND*...................41

Chapter 9: Find Your Strengths................43

Putting Like Tiles Together
Putting odds/evens together

Mini-hands
Multiple Hands
Capitalizing on the Passes

Part V *THE CHARLESTON*..........................47

Chapter 10: Passing Correctly....................49

What to Pass
What not to Pass
Stealing

Chapter 11: Stopping the Charleston........51

When to Stop
Passing after a stopped Charleston

Part VI *STRATEGY*...53

Chapter 12: The Ten Commandments.......55
(Follow these and triple your winnings)

Topics:

The Charleston
Joker exchanges
Discards
Exposures
Hand Selection
Jokerless Mah Jong

Part VII *POINTS TO PONDER*....................59

Chapter 13: Fine Points...............................61

Chapter 14: Decisions................................67

Part VIII THE 2013 CARD..........................71

Chapter 15: The Hands..............................73

Overview
Baby Hands
Near Baby Hands
Special Hands

Part IX *HANDSWITCHING*.........................77

Chapter 16: Handswitches..........................79

Part X *QUIZZES*..83

Chapter 17 : What's the Hand?...................85

Answers to Quizzes

To my mother, Gilda Mallah Grossman, who allowed me to "sit in" on her Mah Jongg games.

Acknowledgemens

To my dear husband Michael D. Fine who patiently helped me with solving the mysteries of the computer and to Betty Malm a devoted friend who encouraged and lent her expertise to editing the manuscript.

Introduction

Congratulations! You have taken the first step toward changing your life for the better.

Mah Jongg is an ancient game played for thousands of years in the Orient. There are numerous books which detail the history and evolution of Mah Jongg; however, the purpose of this book is solely to teach you how to play American Mah Jongg so you can enjoy stimulating and fun times with friends and family.

As an added benefit, your brain will remain forever young! As a long time Mah Jongg teacher, I can attest that I have taught many elderly people and have observed that they become able to think faster and move faster than they did prior to learning the game.

The Five Questions: WHO, WHAT, WHERE, WHEN, HOW?

WHO plays Mah Jongg?

Mah Jongg began in the United States in the 1920's and was standardized by the National Mah Jongg League in 1937. Today, it is played throughout the country primarily by women but men are increasingly joining the ranks. They tend to make excellent players and couples are now enjoying something fun that they can do together.

WHAT is Mah Jongg?

It is a game which is played using Oriental tiles and racks. A Mah Jongg set may be purchased at a game store or on the Internet. Prices vary and a new set will cost about $100.00. A Mah Jongg card is needed and can be obtained from the Mah Jongg League or may be purchased online or from a game store. The cost is $7.00 for a standard sized card and $8.00 for an enlarged card.

WHERE

Most people play in each other's homes using a standard card table. This game is often played in private clubs, recreation centers, senior centers, and country clubs or just about anywhere a flat surface can be found.

WHEN

Anytime

HOW

That's what this book is all about!

PART I
THE EQUIPMENT

Equipment Needed

–> One Mah Jongg Set
–> Four Mah Jongg Cards
–> A Game Table
–> Four Chairs

Mah Jongg cards may be purchased from the National Mah Jongg League. $7.00 for a standard card and $8.00 for a larger one (my recommendation). Send your check to the address listed below OR order your card online.

The National Mah Jongg League
250 West 57th Street
New York, NY 10107

Any questions, go to:
www.nationalmahjonggleague.org

Mah Jongg cards are issued every year around the first of April. So the current year's card is good through March of the following year. Do not buy cards from unknown sources on the Internet. Last year, my students were anxious for the new card and purchased a bogus card online (before the National Mah Jongg League had issued the new cards) and someone made a fortune. Keep in mind that money paid to the League helps the numerous charities that the League supports.

❧ Chapter One ☙
The Mah Jongg Set

Mah Jongg TILES

The Suits
There are three suits:

BAMS 1-9 (4 Each)

CRAKS 1-9 (4 Each)

DOTS 1-9 (4 Each)

Note: The 1 Bam is always a bird. Do not confuse it with a flower!

The Dragons – The Dragons behave exactly as the suits they belong to.

There are three Dragons:

Green (4 each)   **Red** (4 Each)   **White** (4 each)

The Dragons are considered suits –
Green goes with the BAMS
Red goes with the CRAKS
White goes with the DOTS

The Winds

There are four Winds:

NORTH (4 each)   **SOUTH** (4 each)

EAST (4 each)   **WEST** (4 each)

The Flowers (8)
(Ignore the numbers and words on these tiles – all FLOWERS are identical for our purposes)

The Jokers (8)

⋰ CHAPTER TWO ⋱
THE MAH JONGG CARD

The object of Mah Jongg is to make a "hand". Whoever makes a hand first declares "Mah Jongg" and wins the game and usually some money as well. Each year the National Mah Jongg League issues a card listing the hands for that year.

Reading the Mah Jongg Card

The card is arranged by category so that similar hands are grouped together. For example: 2-4-6-

8 hands, 3-6-9 hands, etc. Altogether there are ten categories in the 2013 Mah Jongg card with each hand appearing under its own particular heading (category).

All Hands will have either a red "x" next to the numeric value or the letter "c". The hands with the red "x" means they are exposed hands and the "c" is for concealed. Numeric values and exposed and concealed hands will be further detailed in the section under "game play".

Colors

NOTE: – There are three (3) colors on the card: dark blue, green and red. THE COLORS ON THE CARD HAVE NOTHING TO DO WITH SUIT SELECTION. That choice is yours.

Colors on the card indicate how MANY suits are needed for a particular hand. If you see only all dark blue, it means that particular hand must be made using only one suit. The choice of that suit is up to you.

If you see a hand in green and red it means that particular hand must be made using two suits. The choice of those two suits is up to you. It does NOT mean use BAMS and CRAKS. The colors tell us how many suits we need for any particular hand. Caution: ALWAYS read the fine print next to a hand; the fine print may modify the number of suits and the good thing is it always gives us more ways to make Mah Jongg.

If you see a hand that uses green, red and dark blue it means you need three suits for that hand. The green characters do not mean you should use BAMS for that part of the hand and the red characters do not mean you should use CRAKS for that part of the hand, and the blue characters, oh there is no dark blue Mah Jongg suit (get the point?)

To sum it up simply:
One Color — One Suit

Two colors— Two suits

Three colors — Three suits

YOU choose the suit.

Dragons

The letter "D" on the card means that a dragon is needed.

Just as the numbers in various colors do not indicate which suit to use, a "D" in any color does not tell us which dragon to use. If you see a "D" in red, it does not mean you should use a red dragon. If you see a "D" in green, it does not mean you should use a green dragon, a "D" in dark blue does not mean use a dark blue dragon (of course there are no dark blue dragons). Note: if you happen to see the letter "G" in the color green, it means you must use the green dragon only. If you see the letter "R" in the color red, it means you must use the red dragon. The 2013 Mah Jongg card does not have R's and G's but these have been used in the past.

NEVER FAIL TO READ THE FINE PRINT NEXT TO THE HAND; NOT ONLY DOES THIS PROVIDE CLARIFICATION OF THE HAND BUT ALSO INFORMS US OF ALLOWABLE VARIATIONS OF A HAND.

Special use of WHITE DRAGON for Zero or "0"

In addition to the normal use of White as a dragon, the White also serves as the "0" (zero) in Mah Jongg hands where a zero is required, i.e. the hands that have the current calendar year. When using a White for a zero, it is now a numeric tile and is no longer a dragon therefore it is not a suit. In forming hands using 2013 you may use a 2 and 1 of any suit you like the only caveat is that the 2 and 1 must both be the same suit as each other. . Since our Mah Jongg tiles range from numbers 1 to 9, the question arose how to express the years which contain zeros when there are no zero tiles? Those clever folks at the Mah Jongg League gazed at the White Dragon and decided it sort of resembled a squarish "0" (zero) and voila, a zero was born.

Next to each hand is a numeric value. These values range from 25 to 75. The more difficult the hand, the higher the value. Mah Jongg players generally play for money (not "points"). They use the values on the card to calculate how much a hand is worth. While you may choose to play for thousands of dollars, the usual custom is to play for the value on the card as parts of the dollar. So a hand that has a 25 next to it is a $.25 cent hand. The most expensive hand is the last hand under "singles and pairs" and it is worth $.75 cents. Some folks establish a ceiling on losses. This is called "pie". It means when a player has lost that amount, she plays but does not pay until she gets some money. In my own experience we play for the values on the card for three or four hours and a player seldom loses more than 6 or 7 dollars. A lot of entertainment for a modest amount of money!

Winds and Flowers

The Winds are indicated on the card by the letters "N" "E" "W" "S". The Flowers are indicated by the letter "F". Remember these are NOT suits and are always in dark blue on the card.

Jokers

The card does not ever show where a Joker may be used. Indeed there are some hands which cannot be made without Jokers (e.g., Quint hands) but of course the player will use however many Jokers they wish. The key to using Jokers is simply this; a Joker may only be used for a group of three (3) or more IDENTICAL tiles. Therefore, we may NOT use Jokers for pairs or individual tiles. For example for hands using "2013" no Joker may be used because "2" "0" "1" and "3" are individual tiles.

There is a category of hands called "Singles and Pairs." These represent the most difficult and highest paying hands on the card because no Joker may be used.

To sum up, a Joker can NEVER be used for an individual tile or a pair. There are no exceptions to this rule. For some strange reason new players often will declare Mah Jongg only to expose their hand showing a Joker in a pair When I ask, "don't you know Jokers cannot be used for pairs?" They reply– "it's OK because it was for Mah Jongg!" I know it's tempting but if you need a specific tile for Mah Jongg, a Joker will not help you and you simply discard it (OUCH).

Part II
THE GAME

⊙⊙ Chapter Three ⊙⊙
Getting Started

1. Set up the tiles face down in two layers of nineteen tiles against the flat side of the rack. These are the Mah Jongg walls. The four racks are arranged in a square in front of each player. Leave enough room between the rack and the edge of the table to place the Mah Jongg card.

2. One player is designated as EAST who throws the dice and counts off from the right of her wall setting aside the number of tiles shown on the

dice, e.g. a ten is thrown so ten pairs of tiles are set aside. These tiles are known as the "Hot Wall" and will be the last tiles to be picked unless Mah Jongg is declared before reaching the "Hot Wall."

3. Starting with East each player takes 4 tiles (2 pairs) of tiles in counterclockwise fashion from East's wall. After East's wall is used the wall to East's left (clockwise) is pushed out and the players continue to draw tiles taking 4 tiles at a time until each player has twelve tiles. East then draws 2 tiles by taking the next top tile and the third top tile. The other three players draw one tile each taking the successive tiles.

4. Hand set-up: The tiles are placed on the inside of the racks facing the player. The players examine their tiles and endeavor to find potential hands to play. This is done by putting together their like tiles and tiles that are related to their like tiles and then they must decide which three tiles to eliminate for their first pass to the player to the right.

5. The Charleston. Each player must pass three tiles to the right, across, and left to complete

the first Charleston. For the second Charleston each player passes three tiles to the left, across and to the right. The second Charleston may be omitted if any player wishes to stop after the first Charleston. During the final pass for each Charleston, a player may "steal" one, two or three tiles from the incoming tiles. Players elect to "steal" tiles because they want to withdraw fewer than three tiles from their hands. YOU MAY NOT LOOK AT THE STOLEN TILE(S). Stolen tiles are those that are being passed to you and instead of taking them, you pass them to the left in the first Charleston and to the right in the second Charleston.

6. Courtesy Pass. After the Charleston the players sitting opposite each other may exchange up to three tiles. Defensive Hint: You may not wish to exchange any tiles with an opposite player who has stopped the Charleston.

❧ Chapter Four ❧
Game Play

1. Set up "walls" against the four racks (19 layers of two tiles) See illustration.

2. The player designated as "East" throws the dice and counts off this number of tiles from the right side of her wall and sets them aside.

3. Beginning with East players draw 4 tiles (two rows of two tiles) for 3 rounds in counterclockwise fashion (Walls are pushed out clockwise)

4. East draws two tiles (the top 1st and 3rd tile) for a total of 14 tiles.

5. The remaining players draw 1 tile for a total of 13 tiles.

6. **The Charleston begins**:

Round 1: Three tiles are passed, Right, Across, Left.

Round 2: Three tiles are passed, Left, Across, Right.

Note: *A player may request to stop the Charleston after Round 1; also, a tile may be stolen in Round 1 during the first left and again in Round 2 during the last right.*

7. East begins the game by discarding a tile (remember East had 14 tiles at the outset while the other 3 players drew only 13 tiles.) Player to East's right (counterclockwise) draws the next tile from the wall to East's left. (clockwise)

8. Players pick and discard tiles until someone declares "Mah Jongg." Player names the tile being discarded. If no one declares Mah Jongg, then it is a "wall game" and no one wins.

9. Calling a tile. (For Exposure) A tile is "called" if a player wants another's discard. If you are playing a hand which has a small, red "x" next to the value of the hand, then you may "call" a tile. Player says "Call" and takes the tile from the table and must expose (place on the top of her rack) the called tile along with the other tiles for that portion of the hand. For example, if the player needs four 8 cracks, she must be able to "expose" all four 8 cracks including the one she has "called". (Tiles may NOT be called for exposure from hands having a "c" in front of the value of the hand; however a tile may be called

for a concealed hand IF it's for Mah Jongg.) Jokers may be used for exposure. Tiles may only be called for exposure to complete pungs (three of a kind), kongs (four of a kind) or quints (5 of a kind) or sextet (six of a kind) A tile can NEVER be called to complete a pair unless it is for Mah Jongg.

If an exposure contains jokers, a player may exchange the joker(s) with the real tile(s) on that player's turn, (i.e, the player has picked a tile or called a tile and has not yet discarded). There is no limit to how many jokers may be exchanged during the player's turn.

When a player has completed their hand (has the necessary 14 tiles needed) Mah Jongg is declared. This will happen when that player has picked her final tile for the hand she is playing.

The player then exposes her hand and the Mah Jongg is verified. It is important for the other players NOT to expose their hands until Mah Jongg is verified. If a player has declared Mah Jongg in error, only players whose hands are intact may continue playing.

PART III
RULES OF THE GAME

The rules discussed in this chapter will be confined to the rules set forth by the National Mah Jongg League, Inc. Oftentimes players enjoy modifying the game for various reasons and these are known as "table rules" and need not concern us. All Mah Jongg tournaments are played according to the rules established by the Mah Jongg League and the nice thing about learning these rules and playing that way is that even new players with a little practice can experience the fun of playing in a tournament! Unless you are obsessed with being the top prizewinner, you can have one helluva stimulating and exciting experience just by being a participant. No one knows nor cares about errors you may make in manipulating your hand as long as you "keep up", (i.e., don't hold up the game).

CHAPTER FIVE
SEQUENCE OF PLAY

After the first Charleston is completed a player may want to stop the Charleston, if so, then no second Charleston is played but players may still do a "courtesy " pass in which opposite players may exchange up to three tiles. A courtesy pass will then immediately follow the first Charleston.

Someone called a tile and discarded, whose turn is it now? Answer: The person to the immediate right of the discarder—we do NOT return to the previous order.

After a game is completed, the person to East's right becomes East for the next game. This pattern (counterclockwise) continues throughout game play.

Tiles may be stolen on the first left and on the last right only.

NEVER pick a tile until the person before you has named and discarded a tile.

⋙ Chapter Six ⋘
Called Tiles

1. A tile must be called BEFORE the next person has either discarded or racked a tile.

2. If two people want the same tile, the person closer *in turn* to the discarder will get the tile. Exception: if the person further from the discarder wants the tile for Mah Jongg and the person nearer the discarder wants it for exposure, Mah Jongg declarer will get the tile.

3. When calling a tile for exposure, tiles may be added or subtracted from the exposure prior to the discard. Once a tile is discarded, the exposure is final.

4. If there is a joker(s) in the exposure, players may exchange it with a real tile ON THEIR TURN. Your turn commences when you have picked OR have called a tile. At this time you may make as many joker exchanges as you wish.

5. If a tile is named wrong and someone calls the miscalled tile for exposure, the tile is then correctly named and the game continues. If someone calls the miscalled tile for Mah Jongg, the game is over and miscaller pays four times the value of the hand to the person declaring Mah Jongg. Others do not pay.

6. When a player calls a tile, it becomes that player's "turn". The player to the caller's immediate right then draws the next tile.

CHAPTER SEVEN
DEAD HANDS

1. If a player exposes tiles in error, for example, a player exposes tiles for a concealed hand, another player may call this person "dead" and that player ceases to play and the game resumes with the remaining players. Exposed jokers from an incorrectly exposed hand may NOT be exchanged.

2. If a player exposes tiles correctly, but is called dead for another reason, for example, it is clear from tiles already discarded or exposed that no hand can be made, the player ceases to play BUT the exposed jokers remain viable and may be exchanged.

3. A player may be declared "dead" by another player for a variety of reasons. Under NO circumstances does a player ever declare oneself

to be dead. While the primary goal of Mah Jongg is to win the game, the secondary goal is to prevent another player from getting Mah Jongg. By eliminating yourself from the game you will have made it easier for the remaining players to achieve Mah Jongg. Therefore if no one declares you dead, you should continue to play defensively thereby decreasing the chances for opponents to win.

What does it mean to be dead and what if someone says I am but I know I'm not? If your hand is declared dead and you agree, then you cease playing but the other players continue. If you disagree, then you continue to play and the issue is resolved after the game is over.

It is to your advantage to declare another player dead, but be sure of your ground before doing so. A player may be declared dead if:

Player has too many or too few tiles.

Based on player's exposures and discarded tiles, player cannot make ANY hand. Note: A player is not dead if you are holding tiles player must have to make Mah Jongg.

Question: I call a player dead but that player insists the hand is not dead, what happens?

Answer: Play continues and the issue is resolved at the end of the game. Erring player pays other player lowest hand value. When a player declares Mah Jongg, do NOT immediately expose your hand. Verify that the Mah Jongg is legitimate. If it has been declared in error, those with UNEXPOSED hands continue to play.

CHAPTER EIGHT
DISCARD/EXPOSURE RULES

1. A tile is considered "discarded" if player has "announced" the tile name (EVEN IF THAT TILE IS STILL IN THE PLAYER'S HAND!) or the player has placed the tile on the game table. The player may NOT retract the tile nor may the player exchange the tile for an exposed joker.

2. You have begun to pick a tile and have actually "touched" the tile but then you decide you want to call the tile that was last discarded--Can you put the tile back? NO! Once you have touched or taken a tile even if you haven't "looked" at it, you may not call a tile. It is important not to pick or touch a tile until the person before you has discarded.

If a player miscalls a tile and someone calls that tile for exposure, the tile is correctly named and the game continues.

If a player miscalls a tile and someone calls it for Mah Jongg, the game ends and miscaller pays 4x the value of the hand.

PART IV
SETTING UP A HAND

As a Mah Jongg teacher I can tell you that what I hear most from my students is that their primary trouble is figuring out which hand to play. I always tell them that's the second hardest thing to do in Mah Jongg. "What's the first?", they ask. The answer is "hand switching". In setting up your hand you have the luxury of time and can rearrange your hand before the Charleston begins and during the Charleston there is ample time to find and rearrange hands. Once the game begins, you are expected to pick and throw in a timely manner so any handswitching must be done rapidly.

The question remains, how should I set up my hand when I first get my tiles? From observing my students I have learned what NOT to do. New students invariably set up their tiles by putting their suits together but are still perplexed as to which hand to play!

The reason is the card has NUMERICAL patterns so although you may have put all of your 4 dots and 9 dots together and 3 bams and 8 bams together, you are no closer to finding a hand because no hand exists that use these numeric combinations.

Chapter Nine
Find your strengths

1. Put your "like" tiles together. Even if you only have one pair--find other tiles that can be used with that pair. If you have more than one pair, look for a hand that can utilize both of them. Of course if you have three or four identical tiles, these are super strengths and you definitely should try to form a hand with these. Put these tiles and jokers on the left side of your rack to "save". Save your flowers as well; even if you only have one.

2. If you have no pairs whatsoever, look for other "strengths"-e.g., three different dragons, three different winds, many 3's, 6's. and 9's.

3. BIG TIP: If you have no pairs and can see no strengths, put together all your odd numbered tiles and your even numbered tiles and save which ever you have more of.

4. Look for "mini-hands"— even if you have only 3 tiles for a hand, save those tiles.

5. Often you will not have a clear-cut hand before the Charleston begins, so put together more than one "mini-hand".

6. Be aware of what's being passed. If after the Charleston begins, you seem to be getting similar tiles with each pass, be flexible and capitalize on the tiles you are getting.

7. When deciding on a hand, choose hands that do not require pairs (unless you have the pair). This is especially true if you have several jokers--if the hand requires a pair you will have "wasted" your jokers if you are unable to obtain the needed pair.

8. Do not keep going for the same hands--this is self-sabotage. Go for the hand which give you the most tiles toward Mah Jongg. If you must choose between two hands, go for the easier one. For example, if you have the same number of tiles for an exposed hand as you do for a concealed one, choose the exposed one.

9. By the time the Charleston is completed, you should not be focusing on more than two hands

as this will not only delay your game play but may cause you to make errors.

10. Know the Card. Don't try to memorize every hand, but do know the hand categories. Familiarize yourself with the "baby hands" found in Chapter 15.

Part V
THE CHARLESTON

CHAPTER TEN
PASSING CORRECTLY

1. It is illegal to pass Jokers.

2. While it is legal to pass flowers, it is best avoided if possible as many hands use flowers and passing flowers is not consistent with competitive play.

3. Try to avoid passing pairs, never pass three of the same tile.

4. Do not hesitate to "steal" (permitted on first left and last right} thereby retaining valuable tiles.

Chapter Eleven
Stopping the Charleston

1. You have the option of stopping the Charleston after the first Charleston has been completed (Right-Cross-Left). I have seen Mah Jongg books that (wrongly) advise a player to stop the Charleston if they have two hands and can't decide which one to play.

2. I strongly disagree with the above. Unless you have one fabulous hand (10 or more tiles into Mah Jongg) you should continue to pass tiles. If you have 5 tiles into one hand and 6 tiles into another, in fact you have two weak hands. It is better to choose one hand and continue. By stopping the Charleston you will have eliminated getting up to 12 new tiles with which to improve your hand.

3. If the person opposite you has stopped the Charleston and now offers you tiles for a courtesy pass, you should decline to give any. Obviously you would not want to "help" a person who undoubtedly has an excellent hand. The only exception to this would be that you, in fact, have 10 or more tiles toward making Mah Jongg, and then by all means, do a courtesy pass.

PART VI
STRATEGY

Now that you know how to play Mah Jongg, it is important to learn the various strategies to maximize your odds of winning. Mah Jongg is definitely NOT simply a game of "pick and throw" and those who make lucky picks will win. Strategies are not rules but suggestions for playing smarter. Ultimately your own judgement and experience will guide you and suggestions should be just that. They are guidelines not rules set in stone. Follow them when it makes sense but do not blindly cling to them. The best Mah Jongg players are those who have the flexibility to change course quickly and to take risks when it seems prudent.

The following is a list of some fundamentals,

which will enhance your chances for success. In time you will know when it is wise to risk discarding a dangerous tile and when it would be foolhardy to do so.

CHAPTER TWELVE
THE TEN COMMANDMENTS TO FOLLOW TO BEAT THE COMPETITION.

STRATEGIES

1. If the person sitting opposite you has stopped the Charleston but then requests tiles be exchanged for the courtesy pass, it is wisest NOT to exchange any tiles whatsoever. Obviously this person is probably close to having Mah Jongg already therefore why should you provide additional tiles to potentially improve such a good hand. However, if you are three or fewer tiles from making Mah Jongg yourself, then you might consider doing a courtesy pass.

2. Always try to avoid passing tiles in the Charleston that are pairs or even worse pungs, or three tiles that could easily be used for a hand,

e.g. three dragons. Try to avoid passing flowers—if you must pass a flower, pass them one at a time. Since so many hands contain flowers, it is a kind of gift if passed in the Charleston.

3. Do not do joker exchanges at the end of the game if doing so means the exposures no longer contain jokers. Keep in mind if that player subsequently declares Mah Jongg and has no additional jokers, then all players must pay double the value of the hand since exchanged jokers made the hand jokerless. Of course if taking a player's final exposed Joker gives you Mah Jongg, take it by all means!

4. Do not discard a tile at the end of the game that has not already been discarded unless you can account for three of them. (Tiles are in your own hand or exposed). This is known as a "hot" tile. A good player will break one's own hand at the end of the game rather than risk discarding a hot tile.

5. Do not discard a tile at any time in the game if it is obvious from a player's exposures that the tile may be all that is needed for Mah Jongg. Remember only one person can Mah Jongg — there is no prize for second place. Defensive play requires you to break your hand. Oftentimes

you may be able to "switch" your hand and use the hot tile for a new hand of your own. Good players seldom "give" Mah Jongg.

6. If you are playing a hand for which a pair is needed and you do not yet have the pair, avoid exposing until you have the pair. Once you expose you are "locked" into making a hand that utilizes your exposure. In other words, don't be in a rush to expose. It's better to keep your options open for a while.

7. Discard flowers early in the game. If you are not using flowers do not wait too long before discarding them because they are often needed to complete Mah Jongg

8. If you believe you are holding a hot tile then discard it as quickly as possible unless it is near the end of the game or someone with two or more exposures needs it.

By discarding the hot tile early in the game chances are the player is not ready to claim it for Mah Jongg and the worse case scenario is that they call it for exposure.

9. When selecting a hand be aware that hands that have no pairs or individual tiles are the simplest to make since jokers may be used in

place of real tiles throughout the hand.

10. Never wait to declare Mah Jongg. It might be tempting to not declare mah jongg if you have only a single joker. By waiting you might be able to make a jokerless Mah Jongg and double the value of the hand; however, by waiting there's a good chance someonelse will declare Mah Jongg first and there can only be one winner. In Mah Jongg he who hesitates is really "lost."

PART VII
POINTS TO PONDER

Although Mah Jongg is not such a difficult game when compared to bridge or even Chess, it does have its share of "fine points" a player must be aware of. The following is a review of those points which I feel every Mah Jongg player should know.

CHAPTER THIRTEEN
FINE POINTS

1. When a tile is called, do NOT put it in your hand (on your rack) but place the tile on top of your rack along with the tiles from your hand for exposure. Remember when a tile is wanted by more than one person, it is the person nearest to the discarder who may claim it. Also exposures need not be placed in any specific order but they must be separated.(Space left between exposures)

2. When a tile(s) is stolen, you may not look at it.

3. Once you have announced the tile you wish to discard, you may not change your mind.

4. If a player discards a tile rather than exchanging it for a joker, that tile is "dead". Another player may NOT pick it up and exchange it for a joker.

5. A joker can only be exchanged on your turn. It is not your turn until you have either picked a tile or called a tile. You may then exchange as many tiles as you can including those from your own rack.

6. If a player declares Mah Jongg but then realizes that she does not have Mah Jongg she may continue only if her hand is intact.

7. Never declare yourself dead--regardless of how it happened.

8. The Charleston cannot be stopped if even one player has picked up their second left.

9. If five people are playing Mah Jongg with the 5th person as the "bettor", that person may not "help" the person they bet on. Their financial fate will be exactly like the person on whom the bet was placed. The bettor has the option of betting on a "wall game" in which no one wins. If the bettor is correct, the four players pay the bettor an amount previously agreed upon.

10. If you have picked ahead or even touched your future tile, you may not call a tile--even if it's for Mah Jongg !!!

11. If a player calls a tile and puts up three tiles

but then realizes she needs four, may she add to her exposure? Yes, as long as she has not yet discarded.

12. What happens if a player calls for a tile and places the exposure on her rack but then decides she does not want to expose, may she take back the exposure? NO! Too late! she already made the commitment.

13. When discarding a Joker, what do you say? You have three choices: "Joker", "Same" or name the tile previously thrown, e.g." 3 Dot". A smart player doesn't want to call attention to the fact that she is discarding Jokers so choice 3 is the smartest way to discard a Joker.

14. A tile may NEVER be called to complete a pair unless it is for Mah Jongg. Singletons may not be called either unless it is for Mah Jongg. Any tile may be called for Mah Jongg, even if the hand is concealed.

15. If a player pulls her own tile for Mah Jongg, she receives double the value of the hand. If a Joker exchange resulted in a Mah Jongg, it is considered self-picked and the player collects double from the other players. If the player has no Jokers in the Mah Jongg hand she receives

double. (It doesn't matter if she previously had Jokers but they became exchanged for real tiles) This excludes hands listed under "Singles and Pairs". The player who "gives" a player Mah Jongg pays double and the remaining players pay the value listed next to the hand. Even the lowest value hand (25) could turn out to be a 100 hand if the Mah Jongg was self-picked and there are no jokers in the Mah Jongg. Player is paid double for self pick and double for jokerless mah jongg.

16. A Joker may be redeemed from a dead hand from exposures that were made BEFORE the hand went dead.

17. If a player goes "out-of-turn" and someone calls the discard for Mah Jongg, the game is over and the out-of-turn player pays 4x the value of the hand; however, if a player calls the discard for exposure it is allowed and game continues.

18. Someone declares a player to be dead but the player insists she is not dead. The game continues and resolved at the end of the game. Whoever was right pays the other player the lowest hand value on the card (25).

19. If someone declares Mah Jongg from a discard but has made an error and another player wanted

that same tile for exposure, the tile remains in the dead hand. HOWEVER, if another player needed that same tile to make Mah Jongg she is entitled to take it and do so.

Mah Jongg may be played with fewer than four people; the Charleston is omitted.

CHAPTER FOURTEEN
DECISIONS

While Mah Jongg is an extremely pleasurable game, hence its popularity, there are endless situations that arise during the game in which the player must make a decision. To add to the difficulty of making the "right" decision, a considerate player will not hold up the game in an effort to make the right decision. I personally know an excellent player who always holds up the game when she cannot decide what hand she should play--when I complain, she responds, "but Claire, you don't know my hand". Of course that is totally irrelevant and the Chinese who invented the game consider this to be extremely rude. Of course if all the players are new and play slowly, then it is appropriate to take time to decide what to do. However, if you want to play with the "big girls" you must keep up or risk their wrath.

Some Mah Jongg "Dilemmas"

Q. *Is it always right to exchange a tile for a joker?*

A. No. If you are near the end of the game and you are too far away to make Mah Jongg and the exchange might make the other player jokerless, don't take it especially if there are now no more tiles available for an exchange --remember there are just 4 of every tile. In the case of a flower, even if you don't need the joker, you might take it to prevent another player from getting that joker. If your flower is the 8th flower, then don't exchange it.

Q. *Someone has two exposures and I'm afraid to throw a tile I know she needs. What do I do?*

A. If it's late in the game, do NOT throw it. If it is relatively early (whole walls still intact), throw it immediately. Hopefully, the player is not ready to declare Mah Jongg and the worst-case scenario is she calls for exposure. With "hot" tiles, it's now or never--either discard immediately or resign yourself to not making Mah Jongg and continue to hold the hot tile. While this is not always possible some cagey Maj players will switch their hands to incorporate the hot tile rather than give up their chance to make Mah Jongg.

Q. *Should I steal a tile to prevent passing a pair?*

A. A great question! Of course since you can't look at the stolen tile it's not a guarantee, but in all probability this strategy would work. Yes, passing pairs is to be avoided particularly in the first Charleston when players are trying different hands. This is a judgement call. I don't think I'd do it in the 2nd Charleston but I certainly might in the first.

Q. *I want to call a tile but it's early in the game and I do not yet have a needed pair, what should I do?*

A. Wait! Once you expose you must be able to use that exposure to make your Mah Jongg. If the exposure will still leave you with alternative hands, you might consider calling it. New players are often eager to call but should consider that they will be gaining one tile but may be closing out their options to switch to other hands if they fail to complete the needed pair.

Q. *I want to call a tile and it's late in the game and I do not have a needed pair, what should I do?*

A. Call it! At the end of the game you must be aggressive. It also might work in your favor since with each call all the "picks" are changed.

Q. *It's very early in the game and a player has three exposures and my discard might give her Mah Jongg. What then?*

A. You would be foolish to discard a "hot" tile to a player with three exposures at any time.

Part VIII
THE 2013 CARD

↜ CHAPTER FIFTEEN ↝
THE HANDS

Overview

Every year a new card is issued by the National Mah Jongg League (see illustration) which lists all of the Mah Jongg hands. The new card comes out about the first of April for the current year. Therefore we will be using the 2013 card through March of 2014. To a new player looking at the card for the first time it can be quite overwhelming. In addition to the numerous hands there is also "fine print" next to many of these hands. To become a good player it is important to read and understand how the fine print modifies the hand. It is always to the player's advantage to understand how to interpret the meaning of these explanations. Invariably the fine print not only clarifies the hand but very often offers allowable variations how a hand may be played. The more options we have of making

Mah Jongg, the greater our chances of success.

To help you learn the hands more quickly I suggest that you familiarize yourself with the categories of hands, e.g., "Consecutive Run" "Quints", etc. There are 10 categories in this year's card. You will always have access to your card during a game so there is no need to memorize each one. It is a good idea to know the more popular (simple hands) to increase your odds of winning.

Baby Hands

I call a hand a "baby hand" if jokers can be used in any part of the hand, i.e., the hand only consists of pungs (three of a kind) kongs (four of a kind) or quints (5 of a kind). There are no pairs or singletons. In these hands you theoretically cannot go dead because even if your tiles are already discarded you can use a joker.

Baby Hands

<u>2-4-6-8</u>	<u>Quints</u>	<u>Consecutive Run</u>
4th Hand	2nd, 3rd, 4th	2nd Hand

<u>1-3-5-7-9</u>	<u>Winds/Dragons</u>	<u>3-6-9</u>
2nd Hand	3rd Hand	2nd Hand
(Both Sides)	4th Hand	3rd Hand

Another group of easy hands I call "near" baby hand if they only have one pair or 1 or 2 singletons.

(Almost)Baby Hands

<u>2013</u>   <u>2-4-6-8</u>   <u>Like Numbers</u>

3rd Hand   6th (Last) Hand   1st Hand

<u>Seven Hands</u>   <u>Quints</u>   <u>Consecutive</u>

All   1st Hand   3rd Hand
5th Hand
6th (Last) Hand

<u>1-3-5-7-9</u>   <u>Winds/Dragons</u>

3rd Hand (Both sides)   1st hand
9th (last) Hand   6th (Last) Hand

<u>3-6-9</u>

4th Hand (Both sides)

Special Hands

There are two hands on the card which are a bit confusing. The last hand under 2013 and the second Quint Hand. In the case of the last 2013 hand the illustrated hand appears in three colors; however, when you read the fine print it says you may use 2 OR 3 suits. In the illustrated hand the

"2013" does not match the dragons but because the fine print allows us to use two suits that means the 2013 can match one of the dragons. The same principle holds in the second Quint Hand. The illustrated Hand shows two suits where the Dragon and Number do not match; however, the fine print says you may use ANY Dragon and ANY Number which means you are allowed to use the same suit for your number and your Dragon.

I also want to point out the 3rd and 4th Hand under Winds and Dragons. Note that the six 1's and the six 2's are all in the same color. That means you need SIX of the same tile! You'd better have jokers because there are only 4 of each tile (except of course for Flowers and Jokers).

Part IX
HANDSWITCHING

Chapter Sixteen
Handswitches

As I have mentioned before the most difficult aspect of Mah Jongg is switching your hand. I have listed some handswitches to help with this most challenging part of the game. which illustrates how to switch from a difficult hand to an easier one. Generally this is what happens to a player. Of course it is also possible that an easier hand was attempted but the player drew tiles which enabled her to play a more difficult hand. So keep in mind that handswitches can work both ways.

PRIMARY HAND	**SWITCH TO**
SINGLES AND PAIRS NN EE WW SS 11 22 33	2013 N EE WWW SSSS 2013
SINGLES AND PAIRS FF 11 22 11 22 11 22	CONSECUTIVE RUN 111 222 111 222 DD
SINGLES AND PAIRS 11 33 55 77 99 11 11	1-3-5-7-9 11 333 5555 777 99
SINGLES AND PAIRS FF 11 22 33 44 55 DD	CONSECUTIVE RUN 11 222 3333 444 55
CONSECUTIVE RUN FF 1111 2222 3333	QUINTS FFFF 11111 22222
CONSECUTIVE RUN FFFF 1111 2222 DD	CONSECUTIVE RUN 111 2222 333 4444
SEVEN HANDS FFFF 2222+55 = 7777	1-3-5-7-9 FFFF 5555 77 9999
2013 FF 2013 1111 3333	CONSECUTIVE RUN FF 1111 2222 3333

WINDS – DRAGONS
FF NNNN EE WW SSSS

WINDS - DRAGONS
NNNN EEEE WWWW SS

SEVEN HANDS
FFFF 1111 + 66 = 7777

CONSECUTIVE RUN
FF 6666 7777 8888

1-3-5-7-9
11 33 11 33 55 1111

1-3-5-7-9
111 3333 333 5555

55 77 55 77 99 5555

555 7777 777 9999

111 3 555 111 3 555

111 3333 333 5555

555 7 999 555 7 999

555 7777 777 9999

2013
FFFF DDD 2013 DDD
N EE WWW SSSS 2013

WINDS AND DRAGONS
FFFF DDDD DD DDDD
NNNN EEEE WWWW SS

CONSECUTIVE RUN
11 222 3333 444 55
55 666 7777 888 99

QUINTS
11111 2222 33333
66666 7777 88888

3-6-9
333 666 9999 9999

LIKE NUMBERS
FF 9999 9999 9999

3-6-9
33 666 33 666 9999

3-6-9
333 666 9999 9999

CONSECUTIVE RUN
1111 22 22 22 3333

CONSECUTIVE RUN
FF 1111 2222 3333

1-3-5-7-9
1111 33 55 77 9999
1111 33 55 77 9999

1-3-5-7-9
111 3 555 111 3 555
555 7 999 555 7 999

1-3-5-7-9
11 333 DDDD 333 55
55 777 DDDD 777 99

1-3-5-7-9
111 3333 333 5555
555 7777 777 9999

WINDS – DRAGONS
FF DDDD NEWS DDDD

QUINTS
NNNNN DDDD 11111

QUINTS
1223 22222 22222

LIKE NUMBERS
FF 2222 2222 2222

QUINTS
NNNNN DDDD 11111

WINDS AND DRAGONS
NNNN SSSS 111 111

Part X
Quizzes

CHAPTER SEVENTEEN
WHAT'S THE HAND?

Mah Jongg is a competitive game. The player who only focuses on her own hand and does not pay attention to other player's exposures will often be discarding a tile that will result in another player declaring "Mah Jongg ". The other players will often be angered by this because they will have to pay the declarer as well. I have sat at many a table where the outraged players will cry out, "why did you throw that tile?" It's one thing to take a "risk" in the early part of the game, but if a player has two exposures and you are well into the game, it is foolhardy to discard a dangerous tile. If a player only has one exposure it is generally impossible to figure out what hand is being played. When there are two exposures it is imperative that you know which hand is being played. Sometimes we can only narrow it down to two choices rather than one, but to not have the least idea of what the player is doing is to play like an amateur indeed.

The hands listed below represent two exposures. See if you can determine what hand is being played. Remember these are "exposures", so they cannot be concealed hands.

What's The Hand?

Quiz 1
1. 222 (Crak) 8888 (Bam)
2. 333 (Dot) DDDD (Green)
3. 1111 (Crak) 3333 (Bam) - Two possibilities
4. 4444 (Dot) 6666 (Crak) - Two possibilities
5. 2222 (Bam) DDDD (White)

Quiz 2
1. 666 (Dot) 888 (Dot)
2. 2222 (Crak) DDDD (White)
3. 8888 (Crak) 8888 (Bam) - Two possibilities
4. 777 (Dot) 8888 (Dot)
5. 5555 (Bam) 7777 (Bam)

Answers to Quiz 1

1. 4th Hand under 2-4-6-8
2. 4th Hand under 1-3-5-7-9
3. 5th Hand under Consecutive Run OR 2nd Hand under 2013
4. 2nd Hand under Consecutive Run OR 5th Hand under Consecutive Run
5. 3rd Hand under 2013

Answers to Quiz 2

1. 1st Hand under Consecutive Run (Right Side)
2. 3rd Hand under 2013
3. 2nd Hand under 2-4-6-8 OR 1st Hand under Like Numbers
4. 2nd Hand under Consecutive Run
5. 4th Hand under Consecutive Run

Made in the USA
San Bernardino, CA
08 January 2015